Diaper Covers
Book 2

Crochet 6 super-easy sets for sizes 3-6 months!

2

8

14

20

28

36

LEISURE ARTS, INC. • Maumelle, Arkansas

PANDA SET

 **BEGINNER +**

SHOPPING LIST

Yarn (Medium Weight)
**[7 ounces, 364 yards
(198 grams, 333 meters)
per skein]:**
- ☐ White - 1 skein
- ☐ Black - 25 yards (23 meters)

Crochet Hook
- ☐ Size I (5.5 mm)
  or size needed for gauge

Additional Supplies
- ☐ 1-1¹/₄" (25-32 mm) Button
- ☐ Snaps - 2 **or** 6 (to make the diaper cover adjustable)
- ☐ Yarn needle
- ☐ Sewing needle and matching thread
- ☐ Black felt
- ☐ Craft glue

SIZE INFORMATION

Size: 3-6 months
Finished Measurements:
   Diaper Cover - 14¹/₂" (37 cm) long with an adjustable waist
   Hat - 15" (38 cm) circumference

GAUGE INFORMATION

6 dc and 4 rows/rnds = 2" (5 cm)
Gauge Swatch: 3¹/₄" wide x 3" high (8.25 cm x 7.5 cm)
With White, ch 11.
Row 1: Dc in third ch from hook and in each ch across: 9 dc.
Rows 2-6: Ch 2 (does **not** count as a dc), turn; dc in first dc and in each dc across.
Finish off.

STITCH GUIDE

DOUBLE CROCHET 2 TOGETHER *(abbreviated dc2tog)* (uses 2 sts)

★ YO, insert hook in **next** st, YO and pull up a loop, YO and draw through 2 loops on hook; repeat from ★ once **more**, YO and draw through all 3 loops on hook (**counts as one dc**).

INSTRUCTIONS
Diaper Cover

With White and beginning at waist, ch 67.

Row 1 (Right side)**:** Dc in third ch from hook and in each ch across: 65 dc.

Note: Loop a short piece of yarn around any stitch to mark Row 1 as **right** side.

Row 2: Ch 2 (does **not** count as a dc, now and throughout), turn; dc in first dc and in each dc across.

Row 3 (Buttonhole row)**:** Ch 2, turn; dc in first dc, ch 1, (skip next dc, dc in next 3 dc, ch 1) twice, skip next dc, dc in next 45 dc, ch 1, (skip next dc, dc in next 3 dc, ch 1) twice, skip next dc, dc in last dc: 59 dc and 6 buttonholes (ch-1 sps).

Row 4: Ch 2, turn; dc in first dc and in each dc and in each ch-1 sp across: 65 dc.

Row 5: Ch 2, turn; dc in first dc and in each dc across.

Row 6: Turn; slip st loosely in first 18 dc, ch 2, dc in next 29 dc, leave remaining 18 dc unworked: 29 dc.

Rows 7-13 (Decrease rows)**:** Ch 2, turn; beginning in first dc, dc2tog, dc in next dc and in each dc across to last 2 dc, dc2tog: 15 dc.

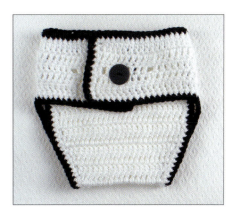

Rows 14 and 15: Ch 2, turn; dc in first dc and in each dc across.

Rows 16-20 (Increase rows)**:** Ch 2, turn; 2 dc in first dc, dc in next dc and in each dc across to last dc, 2 dc in last dc: 25 dc.

Rows 21-28: Ch 2, turn; dc in first dc and in each dc across; do **not** finish off.

EDGING

Rnd 1: Ch 1, do **not** turn; sc evenly around entire piece *(Fig. 5b, page 46)* working 3 sc in each corner; join with slip st to first sc, finish off.

Rnd 2: With **right** side facing, join Black with sc in same st as joining *(Figs. 2a & b, page 44)*; sc in next sc and in each sc around working 3 sc in each corner sc; join with slip st to first sc, finish off.

BUTTONS & SNAPS PLACEMENT

With **right** side facing, sew button to center of Row 26 (front). The front can be buttoned in any of the 3 buttonholes on each side for an adjustable fit.

Snaps are added to keep the corners of the last row in place. Sew a half snap on the **right** side of each corner of Row 28.

Button the diaper cover in the desired position, then sew the second half of each snap on the **wrong** side of Row 1 to correspond with the first half of the snap.

For the diaper cover to be adjustable, the second half of 2 additional snaps may be sewn on each side of Row 1 to match the first half of the snap when the cover is buttoned in the remaining 2 buttonhole choices.

Hat

With White, ch 4; join with slip st to form a ring.

Rnd 1 (Right side)**:** Ch 2 (does **not** count as a dc, now and throughout), 12 dc in ring; join with slip st to first dc.

Note: Mark Rnd 1 as **right** side.

Rnd 2: Ch 2, do **not** turn; 2 dc in same st as joining and in each dc around; join with slip st to first dc: 24 dc.

Rnd 3: Ch 2, dc in same st as joining, 2 dc in next dc, (dc in next dc, 2 dc in next dc) around; join with slip st to first dc: 36 dc.

Rnd 4: Ch 2, dc in same st as joining and in next 2 dc, 2 dc in next dc, (dc in next 3 dc, 2 dc in next dc) around; join with slip st to first dc: 45 dc.

Rnd 5: Ch 2, dc in same st as joining and in each dc around; join with slip st to first dc.

Repeat Rnd 5, 7 times **or** until Hat measures desired length.

Edging: Ch 1, sc in same st as joining and in each dc around; join with slip st to first sc, finish off.

EYE (Make 2)

With White, ch 4; join with slip st to form a ring.

Rnd 1 (Right side)**:** Ch 2, 11 dc in ring; join with slip st to first dc, finish off leaving a long end for sewing.

Note: Mark Rnd 1 as **right** side.

EYE PATCH (Make 2)

With Black, ch 7.

Rnd 1 (Right side)**:** 5 Dc in third ch from hook, dc in next 3 chs, 5 dc in last ch; working in free loops of beginning ch *(Fig. 5b, page 46)*, dc in next 3 chs; join with slip st to first dc: 16 dc.

Note: Mark Rnd 1 as **right** side.

Rnd 2: Ch 2, do **not** turn; 2 dc in same st as joining and in each of next 4 dc, dc in next 3 dc, 2 dc in each of next 5 dc, dc in last 3 dc; join with slip st to first dc, finish off leaving a long end for sewing: 26 dc.

NOSE

With Black, ch 4; join with slip st to form a ring.

Rnd 1 (Right side)**:** Ch 1, 8 sc in ring; join with slip st to first sc, finish off leaving a long end for sewing.

Note: Mark Rnd 1 as **right** side.

EAR (Make 2)

With Black, ch 4; join with slip st to form a ring.

Center (Right side)**:** Ch 2, 12 dc in ring; join with slip st to first dc.

Note: Mark Rnd 1 as **right** side.

Row 1: Ch 2, do **not** turn; 2 dc in same st as joining and in each of next 9 dc, leave remaining 2 dc unworked; do **not** join, finish off leaving a long end for sewing: 20 dc.

Using photo as a guide for placement and long ends, sew one Eye on each Eye Patch, then sew Eye Patches and Nose to Hat. Sew each end of Row 1 and unworked dc on Center of Ears across Rnds 3-5 of Hat.

Cut 2 small circles from Black felt and glue to Eyes.

FROG SET

■□□□ BEGINNER **+**

SHOPPING LIST

Yarn (Medium Weight)

[7 ounces, 364 yards (198 grams, 333 meters) per skein]:
- ☐ Green - 1 skein
- ☐ White - 6 yards (5.5 meters)
- ☐ Black - 2 yards (2 meters)

Crochet Hook
- ☐ Size I (5.5 mm)
  or size needed for gauge

Additional Supplies
- ☐ 1-1¼" (25-32 mm) Button
- ☐ Snaps - 2 **or** 6 (to make the diaper cover adjustable)
- ☐ Yarn needle
- ☐ Sewing needle and matching thread

SIZE INFORMATION

Size: 3-6 months

Finished Measurements:

Diaper Cover - 14¹/₂" (37 cm) long with an adjustable waist

Hat - 15" (38 cm) circumference

GAUGE INFORMATION

6 dc and 4 rows/rnds = 2" (5 cm)

Gauge Swatch: 3¹/₄" wide x 3" high (8.25 cm x 7.5 cm)

With Green, ch 11.

Row 1: Dc in third ch from hook and in each ch across: 9 dc.

Rows 2-6: Ch 2 (does **not** count as a dc), turn; dc in first dc and in each dc across.

Finish off.

STITCH GUIDE

DOUBLE CROCHET 2 TOGETHER *(abbreviated dc2tog)* (uses 2 sts)

★ YO, insert hook in **next** st, YO and pull up a loop, YO and draw through 2 loops on hook; repeat from ★ once **more**, YO and draw through all 3 loops on hook (**counts as one dc**).

INSTRUCTIONS
Diaper Cover

With Green and beginning at waist, ch 67.

Row 1 (Right side)**:** Dc in third ch from hook and in each ch across: 65 dc.

Note: Loop a short piece of yarn around any stitch to mark Row 1 as **right** side.

Row 2: Ch 2 (does **not** count as a dc, now and throughout), turn; dc in first dc and in each dc across.

Row 3 (Buttonhole row)**:** Ch 2, turn; dc in first dc, ch 1, (skip next dc, dc in next 3 dc, ch 1) twice, skip next dc, dc in next 45 dc, ch 1, (skip next dc, dc in next 3 dc, ch 1) twice, skip next dc, dc in last dc: 59 dc and 6 buttonholes (ch-1 sps).

Row 4: Ch 2, turn; dc in first dc and in each dc and in each ch-1 sp across: 65 dc.

Row 5: Ch 2, turn; dc in first dc and in each dc across.

Row 6: Turn; slip st loosely in first 18 dc, ch 2, dc in next 29 dc, leave remaining 18 dc unworked: 29 dc.

Rows 7-13 (Decrease rows)**:** Ch 2, turn; beginning in first dc, dc2tog, dc in next dc and in each dc across to last 2 dc, dc2tog: 15 dc.

Rows 14 and 15: Ch 2, turn; dc in first dc and in each dc across.

Rows 16-20 (Increase rows)**:** Ch 2, turn; 2 dc in first dc, dc in next dc and in each dc across to last dc, 2 dc in last dc: 25 dc.

Rows 21-28: Ch 2, turn; dc in first dc and in each dc across; do **not** finish off.

EDGING

Rnd 1: Ch 1, do **not** turn; sc evenly around entire piece *(Fig. 5b, page 46)* working 3 sc in each corner; join with slip st to first sc.

Rnd 2: Ch 1, **turn**; sc in each sc around working 3 sc in each corner sc; join with slip st to first sc, finish off.

BUTTONS & SNAPS PLACEMENT

With **right** side facing, sew button to center of Row 26 (front). The front can be buttoned in any of the 3 buttonholes on each side for an adjustable fit.

Snaps are added to keep the corners of the last row in place. Sew a half snap on the **right** side of each corner of Row 28.

Button the diaper cover in the desired position, then sew the second half of each snap on the **wrong** side of Row 1 to correspond with the first half of the snap.

For the diaper cover to be adjustable, the second half of 2 additional snaps may be sewn on each side of Row 1 to match the first half of the snap when the cover is buttoned in the remaining 2 buttonhole choices.

Hat

With Green, ch 4; join with slip st to form a ring.

Rnd 1 (Right side)**:** Ch 2 (does **not** count as a dc, now and throughout), 12 dc in ring; join with slip st to first dc.

Note: Mark Rnd 1 as **right** side.

Rnd 2: Ch 2, do **not** turn; 2 dc in same st as joining and in each dc around; join with slip st to first dc: 24 dc.

Rnd 3: Ch 2, dc in same st as joining, 2 dc in next dc, (dc in next dc, 2 dc in next dc) around; join with slip st to first dc: 36 dc.

Rnd 4: Ch 2, dc in same st as joining and in next 2 dc, 2 dc in next dc, (dc in next 3 dc, 2 dc in next dc) around; join with slip st to first dc: 45 dc.

Rnd 5: Ch 2, dc in same st as joining and in each dc around; join with slip st to first dc.

Repeat Rnd 5, 7 times **or** until Hat measures desired length.

Edging: Ch 1, sc in same st as joining and in each dc around; join with slip st to first sc, finish off.

EYE (Make 2)
FRONT
With Black, ch 4; join with slip st to form a ring.

Rnd 1 (Right side)**:** Ch 1, 8 sc in ring; join with slip st to first sc, finish off.

Note: Mark Rnd 1 as **right** side.

Rnd 2: With **right** side facing, join White with dc in same st as joining *(Fig. 3, page 45)*; dc in same st, 2 dc in next sc and in each sc around; join with slip st to first dc, finish off: 16 dc.

Rnd 3: With **right** side facing, join Green with sc in same st as joining *(Figs. 2a & b, page 44)*; 2 sc in next dc, (sc in next dc, 2 sc in next dc) around; join with slip st to first sc, finish off: 24 sc.

BACK
With Green, ch 4; join with slip st to form a ring.

Rnd 1 (Right side)**:** Ch 2, 12 dc in ring; join with slip st to first dc.

Note: Mark Rnd 1 as **right** side.

Rnd 2: Ch 2, turn; 2 dc in same st as joining and in each dc around; join with slip st to first dc, finish off leaving a long end for sewing: 24 dc.

With **wrong** sides of Front and Back together and using long end, sew around entire edge to join. Using photo as a guide for placement, sew Eyes to Hat between Rnds 4 and 5.

MOUSE SET

 **BEGINNER +**

SHOPPING LIST

Yarn (Medium Weight)
[3.5 ounces, 190 yards
(100 grams, 174 meters)
per skein**]:**
- ☐ Grey - 2 skeins
- ☐ Pink - 6 yards (5.5 meters)

Crochet Hook
- ☐ Size I (5.5 mm)
  or size needed for gauge

Additional Supplies
- ☐ 1-1$^{1}/_{4}$" (25-32 mm) Button
- ☐ Snaps - 2 **or** 6 (to make the diaper cover adjustable)
- ☐ Yarn needle
- ☐ Sewing needle and matching thread

SIZE INFORMATION

Size: 3-6 months
Finished Measurements:
Diaper Cover - 14$^{1}/_{2}$" (37 cm)
long with an adjustable waist
Hat - 15" (38 cm) circumference

GAUGE INFORMATION

6 dc and 4 rows/rnds = 2" (5 cm)
Gauge Swatch: 3$^{1}/_{4}$" wide x 3" high
(8.25 cm x 7.5 cm)
With Grey, ch 11.
Row 1: Dc in third ch from hook and in each ch across: 9 dc.
Rows 2-6: Ch 2 (does **not** count as a dc), turn; dc in first dc and in each dc across.
Finish off.

STITCH GUIDE

DOUBLE CROCHET 2 TOGETHER *(abbreviated dc2tog)* (uses 2 sts)

★ YO, insert hook in **next** st, YO and pull up a loop, YO and draw through 2 loops on hook; repeat from ★ once **more**, YO and draw through all 3 loops on hook **(counts as one dc)**.

INSTRUCTIONS
Diaper Cover

With Grey and beginning at waist, ch 67.

Row 1 (Right side)**:** Dc in third ch from hook and in each ch across: 65 dc.

Note: Loop a short piece of yarn around any stitch to mark Row 1 as **right** side.

Row 2: Ch 2 (does **not** count as a dc, now and throughout), turn; dc in first dc and in each dc across.

Row 3 (Buttonhole row)**:** Ch 2, turn; dc in first dc, ch 1, (skip next dc, dc in next 3 dc, ch 1) twice, skip next dc, dc in next 45 dc, ch 1, (skip next dc, dc in next 3 dc, ch 1) twice, skip next dc, dc in last dc: 59 dc and 6 buttonholes (ch-1 sps).

Row 4: Ch 2, turn; dc in first dc and in each dc and in each ch-1 sp across: 65 dc.

Row 5: Ch 2, turn; dc in first dc and in each dc across.

Row 6: Turn; slip st loosely in first 18 dc, ch 2, dc in next 29 dc, leave remaining 18 dc unworked: 29 dc.

Rows 7-13 (Decrease rows)**:** Ch 2, turn; beginning in first dc, dc2tog, dc in next dc and in each dc across to last 2 dc, dc2tog: 15 dc.

Rows 14 and 15: Ch 2, turn; dc in first dc and in each dc across.

Rows 16-20 (Increase rows)**:** Ch 2, turn; 2 dc in first dc, dc in next dc and in each dc across to last dc, 2 dc in last dc: 25 dc.

Rows 21-28: Ch 2, turn; dc in first dc and in each dc across; do **not** finish off.

EDGING

Rnd 1: Ch 1, do **not** turn; sc evenly around entire piece *(Fig. 5b, page 46)* working 3 sc in each corner; join with slip st to first sc.

Rnd 2: Ch 1, **turn**; sc in each sc around working 3 sc in each corner sc; join with slip st to first sc, finish off.

BUTTONS & SNAPS PLACEMENT

With **right** side facing, sew button to center of Row 26 (front). The front can be buttoned in any of the 3 buttonholes on each side for an adjustable fit.

Snaps are added to keep the corners of the last row in place. Sew a half snap on the **right** side of each corner of Row 28.

Button the diaper cover in the desired position, then sew the second half of each snap on the **wrong** side of Row 1 to correspond with the first half of the snap.

For the diaper cover to be adjustable, the second half of 2 additional snaps may be sewn on each side of Row 1 to match the first half of the snap when the cover is buttoned in the remaining 2 buttonhole choices.

Hat

With Grey, ch 4; join with slip st to form a ring.

Rnd 1 (Right side)**:** Ch 2 (does **not** count as a dc, now and throughout), 12 dc in ring; join with slip st to first dc.

Note: Mark Rnd 1 as **right** side.

Rnd 2: Ch 2, turn; 2 dc in same st as joining and in each dc around; join with slip st to first dc: 24 dc.

Rnd 3: Ch 2, turn; dc in same st as joining, 2 dc in next dc, (dc in next dc, 2 dc in next dc) around; join with slip st to first dc: 36 dc.

Rnd 4: Ch 2, turn; dc in same st as joining and in next 2 dc, 2 dc in next dc, (dc in next 3 dc, 2 dc in next dc) around; join with slip st to first dc: 45 dc.

Rnd 5: Ch 2, turn; dc in same st as joining and in each dc around; join with slip st to first dc.

Repeat Rnd 5, 9 times **or** until Hat measures desired length including 2 rnds for a brim.

Edging: Ch 1, sc in same st as joining and in each dc around; join with slip st to first sc, finish off.

EAR (Make 2)

FRONT

With Pink, ch 4; join with slip st to form a ring.

Rnd 1 (Right side)**:** Ch 2, 12 dc in ring; join with slip st to first dc.

Note: Mark Rnd 1 as **right** side.

Rnd 2: Ch 2, do **not** turn; 2 dc in same st as joining and in each dc around; join with slip st to first dc, finish off: 24 dc.

BACK

With Grey, ch 4; join with slip st to form a ring.

Rnd 1 (Right side)**:** Ch 2, 12 dc in ring; join with slip st to first dc.

Note: Mark Rnd 1 as **right** side.

Rnd 2: Ch 2, **turn**; 2 dc in same st as joining and in each dc around; join with slip st to first dc: 24 dc.

Rnd 3: Ch 1, with **wrong** sides of Front and Back together, Back facing and working through **both** layers, sc in same st as joining, 2 sc in next dc, (sc in next dc, 2 sc in next dc) around; join with slip st to first sc: 36 sc.

Rnd 4: Ch 1, **turn**; sc in same st as joining and in next sc, 2 sc in next sc, (sc in next 2 sc, 2 sc in next sc) around; join with slip st to first sc, finish off leaving a long end for sewing: 48 sc.

Using photo as a guide for placement, sew Ears to Hat across Rnds 2-5.

Turn up last 2 rounds of Hat for brim.

BEAR SET

 BEGINNER +

SHOPPING LIST

Yarn (Medium Weight)
[7 ounces, 364 yards
(198 grams, 333 meters) per skein]:
- ☐ Brown - 1 skein
- ☐ Lt Brown - 15 yards
  (13.5 meters)

Crochet Hook
- ☐ Size I (5.5 mm)
  or size needed for gauge

Additional Supplies
- ☐ 1-1¹/₄" (25-32 mm) Button
- ☐ Snaps - 2 **or** 6 (to make the
  diaper cover adjustable)
- ☐ Yarn needle
- ☐ Sewing needle and matching
  thread

SIZE INFORMATION

Size: 3-6 months
Finished Measurements:
   Diaper Cover - 14¹/₂" (37 cm)
      long with an adjustable waist
   Hat - 18" (45.5 cm) circumference

GAUGE INFORMATION

6 dc and 4 rows/rnds = 2" (5 cm)
Gauge Swatch: 3¹/₄" wide x 3" high
   (8.25 cm x 7.5 cm)
With Brown, ch 11.
Row 1: Dc in third ch from hook and
in each ch across: 9 dc.
Rows 2-6: Ch 2 (does **not** count as a
dc), turn; dc in first dc and in each dc
across.
Finish off.

STITCH GUIDE

DOUBLE CROCHET 2 TOGETHER *(abbreviated dc2tog)* (uses 2 sts)

★ YO, insert hook in **next** st, YO and pull up a loop, YO and draw through 2 loops on hook; repeat from ★ once **more**, YO and draw through all 3 loops on hook (**counts as one dc**).

INSTRUCTIONS
Diaper Cover

With Brown and beginning at waist, ch 67.

Row 1 (Right side)**:** Dc in third ch from hook and in each ch across: 65 dc.

Note: Loop a short piece of yarn around any stitch to mark Row 1 as **right** side.

Row 2: Ch 2 (does **not** count as a dc, now and throughout), turn; dc in first dc and in each dc across.

Row 3 (Buttonhole row)**:** Ch 2, turn; dc in first dc, ch 1, (skip next dc, dc in next 3 dc, ch 1) twice, skip next dc, dc in next 45 dc, ch 1, (skip next dc, dc in next 3 dc, ch 1) twice, skip next dc, dc in last dc: 59 dc and 6 buttonholes (ch-1 sps).

Row 4: Ch 2, turn; dc in first dc and in each dc and in each ch-1 sp across: 65 dc.

Row 5: Ch 2, turn; dc in first dc and in each dc across.

Row 6: Turn; slip st loosely in first 18 dc, ch 2, dc in next 29 dc, leave remaining 18 dc unworked: 29 dc.

Rows 7-13 (Decrease rows)**:** Ch 2, turn; beginning in first dc, dc2tog, dc in next dc and in each dc across to last 2 dc, dc2tog: 15 dc.

Rows 14 and 15: Ch 2, turn; dc in first dc and in each dc across.

Rows 16-20 (Increase rows)**:** Ch 2, turn; 2 dc in first dc, dc in next dc and in each dc across to last dc, 2 dc in last dc: 25 dc.

Rows 21-28: Ch 2, turn; dc in first dc and in each dc across; do **not** finish off.

EDGING

Rnd 1: Ch 1, do **not** turn; sc evenly around entire piece *(Fig. 5b, page 46)* working 3 sc in each corner; join with slip st to first sc.

Rnd 2: Ch 1, **turn**; sc in each sc around working 3 sc in each corner sc; join with slip st to first sc, finish off.

BUTTONS & SNAPS PLACEMENT

With **right** side facing, sew button to center of Row 26 (front). The front can be buttoned in any of the 3 buttonholes on each side for an adjustable fit.

Snaps are added to keep the corners of the last row in place. Sew a half snap on the **right** side of each corner of Row 28.

Button the diaper cover in the desired position, then sew the second half of each snap on the **wrong** side of Row 1 to correspond with the first half of the snap.

For the diaper cover to be adjustable, the second half of 2 additional snaps may be sewn on each side of Row 1 to match the first half of the snap when the cover is buttoned in the remaining 2 buttonhole choices.

Rnd 2: Ch 2, do **not** turn; 2 dc in same st as joining and in each dc around; join with slip st to first dc: 24 dc.

Rnd 3: Ch 2, dc in same st as joining, 2 dc in next dc, (dc in next dc, 2 dc in next dc) around; join with slip st to first dc: 36 dc.

Rnd 4: Ch 2, dc in same st as joining and in next 2 dc, 2 dc in next dc, (dc in next 3 dc, 2 dc in next dc) around; join with slip st to first dc: 45 dc.

Hat

With Brown, ch 4; join with slip st to form a ring.

Rnd 5: Ch 2, dc in same st as joining and in each dc around; join with slip st to first dc.

Rnd 1 (Right side)**:** Ch 2 (does **not** count as a dc, now and throughout), 12 dc in ring; join with slip st to first dc.

Note: Mark Rnd 1 as **right** side.

Rnd 6: Ch 2, dc in same st as joining and in next 3 dc, 2 dc in next dc, (dc in next 4 dc, 2 dc in next dc) around; join with slip st to first dc: 54 dc.

Rnd 7: Ch 2, dc in same st as joining and in each dc around; join with slip st to first dc.

Repeat Rnd 7, 5 times **or** until Hat measures desired length.

Edging: Ch 1, sc in same st as joining and in each dc around; join with slip st to first sc, do **not** finish off.

FIRST EAR FLAP

Row 1: Ch 2, do **not** turn; dc in same st as joining and in next 8 sc, leave remaining 45 sc unworked: 9 dc.

Rows 2-4: Ch 2, turn; skip first dc, dc in next dc and in each dc across to last 2 dc, dc2tog: 3 dc.

Finish off.

SECOND EAR FLAP

Row 1: With **right** side of Hat facing, skip next 22 sc from First Ear Flap (front) and join Brown with dc in next sc *(Fig. 3, page 45)*; dc in next 8 sc, leave remaining 14 sc unworked (back): 9 dc.

Rows 2-4: Ch 2, turn; skip first dc, dc in next dc and in each dc across to last 2 dc, dc2tog: 3 dc.

Finish off.

TRIM

With **right** side of Hat facing, join Lt Brown with sc in any sc on Edging at back of Hat *(Figs. 2a & b, page 44)*; sc in each sc on Edging and evenly around Ear Flaps working 3 sc in first and last dc on Row 4 of Flaps; join with slip st to first sc, finish off.

BRAID

Cut 6 strands of both colors, each approximately 24" (61 cm) long.

Holding 3 strands of each color together, pull strands through center sc at bottom of one Ear Flap until ends are even.

Divide the strands into 3 groups of 4 strands each (2 strands of each color) and braid them together; tie end with a overhand knot.

Repeat for second Braid.

EAR (Make 2)
FRONT

With Lt Brown, ch 4; join with slip st to form a ring.

Rnd 1 (Right side): Ch 2, 12 dc in ring; join with slip st to first dc, finish off.

Note: Mark Rnd 1 as **right** side.

Rnd 2: With **right** side facing, join Brown with dc in same st as joining; dc in same st, 2 dc in next dc and in each dc around; join with slip st to first dc, finish off: 24 dc.

BACK

With Brown, ch 4; join with slip st to form a ring.

Rnd 1 (Right side): Ch 2, 12 dc in ring; join with slip st to first dc.

Note: Mark Rnd 1 as **right** side.

Rnd 2: Ch 2, do **not** turn; 2 dc in same st as joining and in each dc around; join with slip st to first dc, finish off leaving a long end for sewing: 24 dc.

With **wrong** sides of Front and Back together and using long end, sew around entire edge to join. Using photo as a guide for placement, sew Ears to Hat across Rnds 3 and 4.

SOCK MONKEY SET

 **BEGINNER +**

SHOPPING LIST

Yarn (Medium Weight)

[3 ounces, 145 yards
(85 grams, 133 meters)
per skein]:
- [ ] Brown - 2 skeins

[3.5 ounces, 170 yards
(100 grams, 156 meters)
per skein]:
- [ ] Red - 1 skein
- [ ] White - 30 yards
  (27.5 meters)

Crochet Hook
- [ ] Size I (5.5 mm)
  or size needed for gauge

Additional Supplies
- [ ] 1-1$^{1}/_{4}$" (25-32 mm) Button
- [ ] Snaps - 2 **or** 6 (to make the
  diaper cover adjustable)
- [ ] Yarn needle
- [ ] Sewing needle and matching
  thread

SIZE INFORMATION

Size: 3-6 months

Finished Measurements:

Diaper Cover - 14$^{1}/_{2}$" (37 cm)
long with an adjustable waist

Hat - 16" (40.5 cm) circumference

GAUGE INFORMATION

6 dc and 4 rows/rnds = 2" (5 cm)

Gauge Swatch: 3$^{1}/_{4}$" wide x 3" high
(8.25 cm x 7.5 cm)

With Brown, ch 11.

Row 1: Dc in third ch from hook and
in each ch across: 9 dc.

Rows 2-6: Ch 2 (does **not** count as
a dc), turn; dc in first dc and in each
dc across.

Finish off.

STITCH GUIDE

DOUBLE CROCHET 2 TOGETHER *(abbreviated dc2tog)* (uses 2 sts)

★ YO, insert hook in **next** st, YO and pull up a loop, YO and draw through 2 loops on hook; repeat from ★ once **more**, YO and draw through all 3 loops on hook (**counts as one dc**).

INSTRUCTIONS
Diaper Cover

With Brown and beginning at waist, ch 67.

Row 1 (Right side)**:** Dc in third ch from hook and in each ch across: 65 dc.

Note: Loop a short piece of yarn around any stitch to mark Row 1 as **right** side.

Row 2: Ch 2 (does **not** count as a dc, now and throughout), turn; dc in first dc and in each dc across.

Row 3 (Buttonhole row)**:** Ch 2, turn; dc in first dc, ch 1, (skip next dc, dc in next 3 dc, ch 1) twice, skip next dc, dc in next 45 dc, ch 1, (skip next dc, dc in next 3 dc, ch 1) twice, skip next dc, dc in last dc: 59 dc and 6 buttonholes (ch-1 sps).

Row 4: Ch 2, turn; dc in first dc and in each dc and in each ch-1 sp across: 65 dc.

Row 5: Ch 2, turn; dc in first dc and in each dc across.

Row 6: Turn; slip st loosely in first 18 dc, ch 2, dc in next 29 dc, leave remaining 18 dc unworked: 29 dc.

Rows 7-13 (Decrease rows)**:** Ch 2, turn; beginning in first dc, dc2tog, dc in next dc and in each dc across to last 2 dc, dc2tog: 15 dc.

Rows 14 and 15: Ch 2, turn; dc in first dc and in each dc across.

Rows 16-20 (Increase rows)**:** Ch 2, turn; 2 dc in first dc, dc in next dc and in each dc across to last dc, 2 dc in last dc: 25 dc.

Rows 21-28: Ch 2, turn; dc in first dc and in each dc across; finish off.

EDGING

Rnd 1: With **wrong** side facing, join White with sc in same st as joining *(Figs. 2a & b, page 44)*; sc evenly around entire piece *(Fig. 5b, page 46)* working 3 sc in each corner; join with slip st to first sc, finish off.

Rnd 2: With **right** side facing, join Red with sc in same st as joining; sc in next sc and in each sc around working 3 sc in each corner sc; join with slip st to first sc, finish off.

BUTTONS & SNAPS PLACEMENT

With **right** side facing, sew button to center of Row 26 (front). The front can be buttoned in any of the 3 buttonholes on each side for an adjustable fit.

Snaps are added to keep the corners of the last row in place. Sew a half snap on the **right** side of each corner of Row 28.

Button the diaper cover in the desired position, then sew the second half of each snap on the **wrong** side of Row 1 to correspond with the first half of the snap.

For the diaper cover to be adjustable, the second half of 2 additional snaps may be sewn on each side of Row 1 to match the first half of the snap when the cover is buttoned in the remaining 2 buttonhole choices.

Hat

With Red, ch 4; join with slip st to form a ring.

Rnd 1 (Right side)**:** Ch 2 (does **not** count as a dc, now and throughout), 12 dc in ring; join with slip st to first dc.

Note: Mark Rnd 1 as **right** side.

Rnd 2: Ch 2, do **not** turn; 2 dc in same st as joining and in each dc around; join with slip st to first dc: 24 dc.

Rnd 3: Ch 2, dc in same st as joining, 2 dc in next dc, (dc in next dc, 2 dc in next dc) around; join with slip st to first dc: 36 dc.

Rnd 4: Ch 2, dc in same st as joining and in each dc around; join with slip st to first dc.

Rnd 5: Ch 2, working in Front Loops Only *(Fig. 4, page 45)*, dc in same st as joining and in each dc around; join with slip st to first dc, finish off.

Rnd 6: With **right** side facing, fold Rnd 5 towards you; working in free loops of Rnd 4 *(Fig. 5a, page 46)*, join Brown with dc in same st as joining *(Fig. 3, page 45)*, dc in next dc, 2 dc in next dc, (dc in next 2 dc, 2 dc in next dc) around; join with slip st to first dc: 48 dc.

Rnds 7-11: Ch 2, working in both loops, dc in same st as joining and in each dc around; join with slip st to first dc.

Finish off.

Rnd 12: With **right** side facing, join White with sc in same st as joining *(Figs. 2a & b, page 44)*, sc in next dc and in each dc around; drop White, with Red, join with slip st to first sc *(Fig. 6, page 46)*.

Rnd 13: Ch 2, dc in same st as joining and in each sc around; cut Red, with White, join with slip st to first dc.

Rnd 14: Ch 1, sc in same st as joining and in each dc around; cut White, with Brown, join with slip st to first sc.

Rnd 15: Ch 2, dc in same st as joining and in each sc around; join with slip st to first dc; do **not** finish off.

FIRST EAR FLAP

Row 1: Ch 2, do **not** turn; dc in same st as joining and in next 8 dc, leave remaining 39 dc unworked: 9 dc.

Rows 2-4: Ch 2, turn; skip first dc, dc in next dc and in each dc across to last 2 dc, dc2tog: 3 dc.

Finish off.

SECOND EAR FLAP

Row 1: With **right** side of Hat facing, skip next 21 dc from First Ear Flap (front) and join Brown with dc in next dc; dc in next 8 dc, leave remaining 9 dc unworked (back): 9 dc.

Rows 2-4: Ch 2, turn; skip first dc, dc in next dc and in each dc across to last 2 dc, dc2tog: 3 dc.

Finish off.

BRAID

Cut 2 strands of all 3 colors, each approximately 24" (61 cm) long.

Holding a strand of each color together, pull strands through center dc on end of Ear Flap, until ends are even.

Divide the strands into 3 groups of 2 strands each of matching color and braid them together; tie end with a overhand knot.

Repeat for second Braid.

EAR (Make 2)

With Brown, ch 4; join with slip st to form a ring.

Row 1: Ch 2, 7 dc in ring.

Row 2: Ch 2, turn; 2 dc in first dc, (dc in next dc, 2 dc in next dc) 3 times; finish off leaving a long end for sewing.

Using photo as a guide for placement and long ends, sew Ears to Hat.

POM-POM

Cut a piece of cardboard 2" (5 cm) square.

Using Red, wind the yarn around the cardboard until it is approximately $^1/_2$" (12 mm) thick in the middle *(Fig. 1a)*.

Carefully slip the yarn off the cardboard and firmly tie an 18" (45.5 cm) length of yarn around the middle *(Fig. 1b)*. Leave yarn ends long enough to attach the pom-pom.

Cut the loops on both ends and trim the pom-pom into a smooth ball *(Fig. 1c)*.

Attach pom-pom to top of Hat.

Fig. 1a

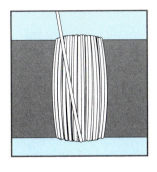

Fig. 1b

Fig. 1c

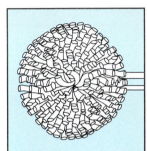

LAMB SET

 **BEGINNER +**

SIZE INFORMATION

Size: 3-6 months
Finished Measurements:
Diaper Cover - $13^1/_2$" (34.5 cm)
long with an adjustable waist
Hat - 16" (40.5 cm) circumference

GAUGE INFORMATION

4 dc = 2" (5 cm) and
3 rows/rnds = $2^1/_2$" (6.25 cm)
Gauge Swatch: 4" wide x $2^1/_2$" high
(10 cm x 6.25 cm)
Ch 10.
Row 1: Dc in third ch from hook and
in each ch across: 8 dc.
Rows 2 and 3: Ch 3 **(counts as first
dc)**, turn; dc in next dc and in each
dc across.
Finish off.

STITCH GUIDE

DOUBLE CROCHET 2 TOGETHER *(abbreviated dc2tog)* (uses next 2 sts)

★ YO, insert hook in **next** st, YO and pull up a loop, YO and draw through 2 loops on hook; repeat from ★ once **more**, YO and draw through all 3 loops on hook **(counts as one dc)**.

INSTRUCTIONS
Diaper Cover

Beginning at waist, ch 44.

Row 1 (Right side)**:** Dc in fourth ch from hook **(3 skipped chs count as first dc)** and in each ch across: 42 dc.

Note: Loop a short piece of yarn around any stitch to mark Row 1 as **right** side.

Row 2 (Buttonhole row)**:** Ch 3 **(counts as first dc, now and throughout)**, turn; dc in next dc, (ch 1, dc2tog) 3 times, dc in next 26 dc, (dc2tog, ch 1) 3 times, dc in last 2 dc: 36 dc and 6 buttonholes (ch-1 sps).

Row 3: Ch 3, turn; dc in next dc and in each dc and in each ch-1 sp across: 42 dc.

Row 4: Turn; slip st loosely in first 13 dc, ch 3, dc in next 17 dc, leave remaining 12 dc unworked: 18 dc.

Rows 5-8 (Decrease rows)**:** Ch 3, turn; dc2tog, dc in next dc and in each dc across to last 3 dc, dc2tog, dc in last dc: 10 dc.

Row 9: Ch 3, turn; dc in next dc and in each dc across.

Rows 10-12 (Increase rows)**:** Ch 3, turn; dc in first dc and in each dc across to last dc, 2 dc in last dc: 16 dc.

Rows 13-16: Ch 3, turn; dc in next dc and in each dc across.

Finish off.

BUTTONS & SNAPS PLACEMENT

With **right** side facing, sew button to center of Row 15 (front). The front can be buttoned in any of the 3 buttonholes on each side for an adjustable fit.

Snaps are added to keep the corners of the last row in place. Sew a half snap on the **right** side of each corner of Row 16.

Button the diaper cover in the desired position, then sew the second half of each snap on the **wrong** side of Row 1 to correspond with the first half of the snap.

For the diaper cover to be adjustable, the second half of 2 additional snaps may be sewn on each side of Row 1 to match the first half of the snap when the cover is buttoned in the remaining 2 buttonhole choices.

Hat

Ch 4; join with slip st to form a ring.

Rnd 1 (Right side)**:** Ch 3 **(counts as first dc, now and throughout)**, 11 dc in ring; join with slip st to first dc: 12 dc.

Note: Mark Rnd 1 as **right** side.

Rnd 2: Ch 3, do **not** turn; dc in same st as joining, 2 dc in next dc and in each dc around; join with slip st to first dc: 24 dc.

Rnd 3: Ch 3, dc in next dc, 2 dc in next dc, (dc in next 2 dc, 2 dc in next dc) around; join with slip st to first dc: 32 dc.

Rnds 4-7: Ch 3, dc in next dc and in each dc around; join with slip st to first dc.

Finish off.

EAR (Make 2)

Ch 12.

Rnd 1: 2 Dc in fourth ch from hook, dc in next 7 chs, 3 dc in last ch; working in free loops of beginning ch *(Fig. 5b, page 46)*, dc in next 7 chs; join with slip st to first dc: 20 dc.

Rnd 2 (Right side)**:** Ch 3, dc in next dc and in each dc around; join with slip st to first dc, finish off leaving a long end for sewing.

Using photo as a guide for placement, sew Ears to Hat between Rnds 3 and 4.

Tie ribbon in a bow around any dc on Rnd 3.

GENERAL INSTRUCTIONS

ABBREVIATIONS

cm	centimeters
ch	chain(s)
dc	double crochet(s)
dc2tog	double crochet 2 together
mm	millimeters
Rnd(s)	Round(s)
sc	single crochet(s)
sp(s)	space(s)
st(s)	stitch(es)
YO	yarn over

SYMBOLS & TERMS

★ — work instructions following ★ as many **more** times as indicated in addition to the first time.

( ) **or [ ]** — work enclosed instructions **as many** times as specified by the number immediately following **or** contains explanatory remarks.

colon (:) — the number(s) given after a colon at the end of a row or round denote(s) the number of stitches or spaces you should have on that row or round.

CROCHET TERMINOLOGY		
UNITED STATES		INTERNATIONAL
slip stitch (slip st)	=	single crochet (sc)
single crochet (sc)	=	double crochet (dc)
half double crochet (hdc)	=	half treble crochet (htr)
double crochet (dc)	=	treble crochet(tr)
treble crochet (tr)	=	double treble crochet (dtr)
double treble crochet (dtr)	=	triple treble crochet (ttr)
triple treble crochet (tr tr)	=	quadruple treble crochet (qtr)
skip	=	miss

CROCHET HOOKS	
Metric mm	U.S.
2.25	B-1
2.75	C-2
3.25	D-3
3.5	E-4
3.75	F-5
4	G-6
5	H-8
5.5	I-9
6	J-10
6.5	K-10½
8	L-11
9	M/N-13
10	N/P-15
15	P/Q
16	Q
19	S

Yarn Weight Symbol & Names	LACE 0	SUPER FINE 1	FINE 2	LIGHT 3	MEDIUM 4	BULKY 5	SUPER BULKY 6
Type of Yarns in Category	Fingering, 10-count crochet thread	Sock, Fingering Baby	Sport, Baby	DK, Light Worsted	Worsted, Afghan, Aran	Chunky, Craft, Rug	Bulky, Roving
Crochet Gauge* Ranges in Single Crochet to 4" (10 cm)	32-42 double crochets**	21-32 sts	16-20 sts	12-17 sts	11-14 sts	8-11 sts	5-9 sts
Advised Hook Size Range	Steel*** 6,7,8 Regular hook B-1	B-1 to E-4	E-4 to 7	7 to I-9	I-9 to K-10.5	K-10.5 to M-13	M-13 and larger

*GUIDELINES ONLY: The chart above reflects the most commonly used gauges and hook sizes for specific yarn categories.

** Lace weight yarns are usually crocheted on larger-size hooks to create lacy openwork patterns. Accordingly, a gauge range is difficult to determine. Always follow the gauge stated in your pattern.

*** Steel crochet hooks are sized differently from regular hooks–the higher the number the smaller the hook, which is the reverse of regular hook sizing.

▰▱▱▱ BEGINNER	Projects for first-time crocheters using basic stitches. Minimal shaping.
▰▰▱▱ EASY	Projects using yarn with basic stitches, repetitive stitch patterns, simple color changes, and simple shaping and finishing.
▰▰▰▱ INTERMEDIATE	Projects using a variety of techniques, such as basic lace patterns or color patterns, mid-level shaping and finishing.
▰▰▰▰ EXPERIENCED	Projects with intricate stitch patterns, techniques and dimension, such as non-repeating patterns, multi-color techniques, fine threads, small hooks, detailed shaping and refined finishing.

GAUGE

Exact gauge is **essential** for proper fit. Before beginning your project, make the sample swatch given in the individual instructions in the yarn and hook specified. After completing the swatch, measure it, counting your stitches and rows carefully. If your swatch is larger or smaller than specified, **make another, changing hook size to get the correct gauge**. Keep trying until you find the size hook that will give you the specified gauge.

JOINING WITH SC

When instructed to join with sc, begin with a slip knot on hook. Insert hook in stitch indicated, YO and pull up a loop, YO and draw through both loops on hook *(Figs. 2a & b)*.

Fig. 2a

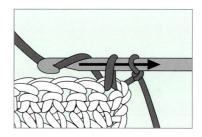

Fig. 2b

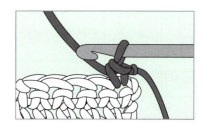

JOINING WITH DC

When instructed to join with dc, begin with a slip knot on hook. YO, holding loop on hook, insert hook in stitch indicated, YO and pull up a loop (3 loops on hook), (YO and draw through 2 loops on hook) twice *(Fig. 3)*.

Fig. 3

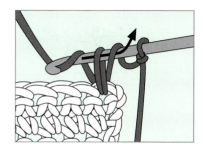

FRONT LOOPS ONLY

Work only in loop(s) indicated by arrow *(Fig. 4)*.

Fig. 4

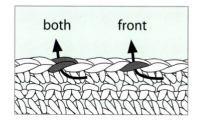

FREE LOOPS

After working in Front Loops Only on a round, there will be a ridge of unused loops. These are called the free loops. Later, when instructed to work in the free loops on the same round, work in these loops *(Fig. 5a)*.

When instructed to work in free loops of a chain, work in loop indicated by arrow *(Fig. 5b)*.

Fig. 5a

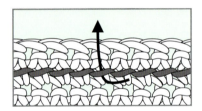

Fig. 5b

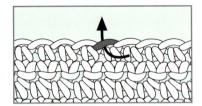

CHANGING COLORS

To change colors at the end of a round while joining with a slip stitch, cut yarn, insert hook in first stitch, with new yarn, YO and draw through stitch and loop on hook *(Fig. 6)*.

Fig. 6

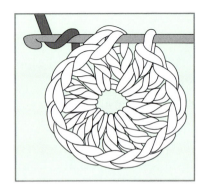

YARN INFORMATION

The projects in this leaflet were made using Medium or Super Bulky Weight Yarn. Any brand of the specific weight of yarn may be used. It is best to refer to the yardage/meters when determining how many balls or skeins to purchase. Remember, to arrive at the finished size, it is the GAUGE/TENSION that is important, not the brand of yarn.

Listed below are the specific yarns used to create our photography models.

PANDA SET

Red Heart® Super Saver®

White - #0311 White

Black - #0312 Black

BEAR SET

Red Heart® Super Saver®

Brown - #0365 Coffee

Lt Brown - #0336 Warm Brown

FROG SET

Red Heart® Super Saver®

Green - #0672 Spring Green

White - #0316 Soft White

Black - #0312 Black

SOCK MONKEY SET

Lion Brand® Vanna's Choice®

Brown - #302 Taupe Mist

Red - #113 Scarlet

White - #100 White

MOUSE SET

Red Heart® Classic®

Grey - #0401 Nickel

Pink - #0719 Lily Pink

LAMB SET

Red Heart® Light & Lofty®

#9334 Café Au Lait

We have made every effort to ensure that these instructions are accurate and complete. We cannot, however, be responsible for human error, typographical mistakes, or variations in individual work.

Production Team: Writer/Technical Editor - Cathy Hardy; Editorial Writer - Susan Frantz Wiles; Senior Graphic Artist - Lora Puls; Graphic Artist - Jessica Bramlett; Photo Stylist - Christy Myers; and Photographer - Ken West.

Instructions tested and photo models made by Lee Ellis.